THE
IDEA
PLAYBOOK

INNOVATION

A SUREFIRE GUIDE TO GENERATE BUSINESS IDEA, AND LAUNCHING IN 21 DAYS FLAT

RAFIAT BABAYODE

The
Idea
Playbook

Rafiat Babayode

CONTENT TABLE

ACKNOWLEDGMENT

This book was an absolute pleasure to write thanks to the support from the amazing MOREMEE community. I want to give a special thanks to all our Moremee Founders. Your support means I can keep running my dream company! I also realize I couldn't have done any of this without the tireless love and support of my husband, Abimbola Akinola. His patience while I wrote this book is amazing. Thanks for putting up with my late-night rants. I want to sincerely thank my mother, for her unwavering love, support, and dedication. During her three-month stay in with me, here in Canada, she not only lovingly cared for my children but also gave me the precious gift of time and tranquility to focus on my writing. Finally, love and thanks to all the families and partners of the Rapid Launch team, who work tirelessly to spread the Idea Generation and Validation word.

B. Rafiat

INTRODUCTION

My Take!

It has always been my passion to see fellow mothers happy.

Do you know why?

I understand what it feels like to be a mother – the challenges, the mental breakdowns, the financial stress, and countless other struggles.

I never anticipated that I would be able to do anything meaningful with my life when I found out I was pregnant with my third child when my second was just 7-month-old. But here I am today:

I am a product manager,

I am a serial entrepreneur,

I have control over my time,

I manage my finances,

I have time for myself,

I have time for my family!

This is the joy I want to share with other mothers.

That's why I'm creating this Idea Playbook.

I am excited to witness a league of women having complete control over their time, experiencing the maximum comfort they seek.

To you, who is reading this right now, I want to offer my sincere congratulations because you have chosen the path of total freedom.

And to be honest with you, it is truly worth it.

Once again, I say big congratulations!

Freedom always comes at a price, and I'm glad you are willing to pay for it by getting your hands on this Idea Playbook.

This book has been crafted based on my many years of experience in entrepreneurship. It covers my journey from becoming a renowned Product Manager to starting and running a successful business that has generated over $40k in revenue in less than a year.

You are about to read about my experiences in this Idea Playbook.

I don't mean to say that you will be reading a story, but I want you to know that this book provides a step-by-step guide to achieving success in entrepreneurship based on my experiences!

I won't talk too much now. Dive into the pages and see the reality for yourself.

In advance, I want to say a big congratulations as you carefully read through this Idea Playbook!

With all my love,

Rafiat B.

DAY 1

Introduction / Overview

Understanding the Challenges of Starting a Business and the Role of This Book in Overcoming Them

Imagine yourself as the owner of a thriving business— one that not only brings you financial success, but also fills your life with a deep sense of purpose and satisfaction.

It is because you believe in the immense potential of such an endeavor, you've embarked on this journey by picking up this book.

You yearn for the freedom that comes from being your own boss and you desire the fulfillment that comes from using your unique skills and talents to make a meaningful impact on the world.

However, you know that there are obstacles standing in your way, preventing you from turning this dream into a reality.

Trust me, I have been there. Starting a business can be a discouraging task if you ask me, and it's not unusual to face various challenges along the way.

Maybe you're not sure of where to start, or you feel overwhelmed by the amount of information and decisions involved in launching a successful venture.

Maybe you lack the necessary resources, be it financial capital, industry connections, or a supportive network. Also, fear and self-doubt might be holding you back, making it difficult to take that crucial first step.

All of these feelings are very normal. You are not alone.

Now this is where this book comes in. You are so going to love this, I promise. Its purpose is to guide you through the complexity of starting a business, helping you move through and overcoming the challenges involved.

By delving into the pages of this book, you will gain valuable insights, practical advice, and actionable strategies to overcome the challenges you're currently facing.

Are you struggling to start the right business?

Or are you struggling to come up with a good business idea?

Or you are feeling overwhelmed by too many ideas and fear of making the wrong choice

Or you doubt the visibility of your idea?

Or is it identifying your target audience, or even increasing your self-confidence?

This book will provide you with the tools and knowledge to achieve all of the above and set you on the path to entrepreneurial success. So, get ready to embark on this transformative journey.

You and I will explore the world of business, unveil the mysteries of entrepreneurship, and equip you with the skills and mindset necessary to build the business of your dreams.

It's time to unleash your potential and embrace the possibilities that await you as a successful business owner.

STRUGGLING TO START THE RIGHT BUSINESS!

There's nothing more frustrating than knowing you have great potential but feeling stuck because you're not sure what business to start. It's like time isn't on your side, and you're left wondering why you haven't made more progress.

I've seen many people dealing with this problem, and I've experienced it myself. I had so many ideas, but I couldn't figure out which one was the best. I'll share more about my own journey later.

The truth is, not knowing what business to pursue can make you feel miserable, frustrated, stressed, and full of self-doubt. It can also waste a lot of your time and potential.

Since I've been through this difficult situation myself and heard from many readers facing the same struggle, I felt the need to help.

That's why I created this playbook: To give you a clear roadmap that helps you make a decision and take action.

It will give you the head start you need to finally start the perfect business for you—a business that is profitable, meaningful, and that you will truly enjoy.

Based on my experience, I've noticed that many aspiring entrepreneurs face one or all of these three main challenges:

STRUGGLING TO COME UP WITH GOOD IDEAS:

"I really want to start my own business, but I'm stuck because I can't think of any solid or unique ideas.

It seems like all the good ones are already taken. How can I generate viable and innovative ideas for my business?"

FEELING OVERWHELMED BY TOO MANY IDEAS AND FEAR OF MAKING THE WRONG CHOICE:

"I have so many passions and interests, and I'm scared to narrow it down to just one.

I don't want to miss out or make the wrong decision for my business.

How can I embrace my various interests while still choosing the right idea to focus on?"

DOUBTS ABOUT THE FEASIBILITY OF THEIR IDEA:

"I have a specific business idea in mind, but I haven't taken the leap yet.

I'm afraid of failure and making costly mistakes.

How can I validate and ensure that my idea is viable before investing a lot of time and resources into it?"

These are the common challenges that entrepreneurs like you often face. I faced it and every other entrepreneurs, so it is normal. But, It is important to address each one in order to move forward confidently and make informed decisions.

If you're facing any of these challenges, you're in the right place.

Before we dive deeper, let's make sure we're completely aligned on this. I want to be clear: this is not a "get rich quick" scheme, and I won't sugarcoat it.

What I'm about to propose won't be easy. Starting and growing a business is demanding, time-consuming, and emotionally draining!

The goal here is to create a real, sustainable, and profitable business that you can take pride in and that can provide financial security for you and your loved ones.

If you choose to move forward, be prepared for hard work and long hours. I'm serious. Success in business requires mental resilience and relentless effort over a long period of time.

Especially at the beginning, you may find yourself working tirelessly for little pay. For many of us, this phase of investing time and effort without immediate rewards can last anywhere from a few months to a few years.

You also need to be ready to face disappointment, rejection, self-doubt, frustration, and sometimes even loneliness along the way.

But here's the exciting part:

No matter how smart, passionate, or prepared you are, and regardless of the hours you put in or how hard you work, there are no guarantees of success.

Hold on, I'm not saying this to discourage you. I am telling you this to empower you. Because here's a truth every aspiring entrepreneur needs to understand:

If you're seeking guarantees in business, you're not really seeking a business. Every business venture carries inherent risks. You have to be willing to risk your money, time, energy, and ego.

None of us can predict with certainty what will work and what won't. Business is an exciting and sometimes challenging game. It requires research, strategy, determination, intuition, creativity, action, and constant adjustments.

You must remain vigilant, adaptable, and committed to personal growth. There are no shortcuts or magical solutions.

Business is a dynamic process of testing ideas, gaining experience, refining your offerings, and building momentum and confidence over time.

 And most importantly, you have to genuinely love this process and your business, you just have to, or you won't survive.

You can read the top 100 business books, seek advice from successful entrepreneurs, or consult various sources, but until you take action, until you take a step, you won't truly know what will work for you.

I hope you appreciate my honesty because to start the right business, you need to understand and accept the realities of the game. Having a clear understanding of the playing field brings you closer to success.

While there are no guarantees in any business, there are ways to position yourself for the best possible outcome. You need to be honest with yourself about your skills, strengths, and work ethic.

And as soon as possible, you need to test your ideas, validate your concepts, and generate revenue.

There are fundamental principles and practices that can guide you to make intelligent and strategic steps towards building momentum and profitability over time.

That's precisely what this playbook aims to teach you and help you achieve. As you put these ideas into action, the objective is to gain clarity, self-awareness, and confidence through small victories and real-world experience.

What you will get out of this?

In this book, you'll gain valuable insights and practical steps to help you start and grow your ideal business. By engaging with the content, you'll achieve the following:

Generating Business Ideas: Tap into your creative potential and learn effective techniques to come up with innovative and viable business ideas.

You'll explore different avenues and discover opportunities that align with your passions and goals.

Selecting the Right Idea: Navigate the process of choosing the best business idea for you. With clarity and confidence, you'll identify the idea that deeply resonates with your values and aspirations, setting the stage for a fulfilling entrepreneurial journey.

Validating Your Idea: Learn how to assess the feasibility and potential success of your chosen business idea. Through practical validation strategies and expert guidance, you'll minimize risks and ensure your idea has a strong foundation before investing significant time and resources.

Decision-Making and Action-Taking: Develop the skills to make clear, informed decisions and take decisive action on your entrepreneurial path. The book equips you with tools and a mindset to overcome challenges, embrace opportunities, and move your business forward. This right here is very important.

Resourceful Growth: Access curated resources, tools, and recommended further reading to deepen your knowledge and support your ongoing growth as an entrepreneur. These resources empower you to expand your skills, stay updated with industry trends, and navigate the changing business landscape.

Confidence and Motivation: Another very important benefit that you get from this book is acquiring a strong sense of confidence and motivation as you embark on your business journey. You know having an idea without the confidence or motivation to push it through, you're stuck. The book provides inspiration, practical advice, and real-life examples to help you overcome obstacles, stay focused, and remain resilient.

In addition, you'll receive a complimentary planner designed to help you implement the strategies effectively. This planner will serve as your dedicated companion, providing structure, organization, and accountability. It includes templates, checklists, and goal-setting exercises to keep you on track, prioritize tasks, and track progress.

By implementing the insights from the book and the planner, you'll have a powerful combination to turn knowledge into action and make meaningful progress toward your entrepreneurial goals.

Get ready to confidently embark on your business journey and transform your dreams into a thriving reality.

What won't you see in this book?

It's important to understand what this playbook doesn't provide. Here are a few things you won't find in its pages:

Ready-Made Business Ideas: Instead of giving you pre-packaged business ideas, this playbook helps you generate and validate your own ideas based on your passions and goals. This book will not force ideas on you, instead, you'll be encouraged to generate your own ideas based on your passion, skills etc.

Overnight Success Formulas: The playbook doesn't promise instant success or offer shortcuts. It is not a magic wand. It focuses on providing tools and strategies to build a strong foundation and navigate challenges over time.

Industry-Specific Advice: While the playbook covers essential principles applicable to various industries, it doesn't offer detailed strategies for specific sectors. Its focus is on foundational aspects that can be applied across different industries.

Financial or Legal Advice: The playbook provides general insights on finances and legal aspects, but it's important to consult with professionals for specific financial and legal advice.

Guaranteed Success: The playbook doesn't guarantee success. It offers valuable knowledge and steps, but your commitment, execution, and external factors also play a role in achieving success.

Remember, this playbook empowers you with knowledge, mindset, and tools to start and grow your business. Your dedication, resilience, and continuous learning will be vital for your entrepreneurial journey.

If you are looking for the easiest and the most profitable online business for moms, click on this link to try out 30-Day Course Moremee.

DAY 2

How Do You Come Up with Ideas for Your Business (I)

If you've been struggling to come up with good ideas for your business, this lesson is perfect for you. The good news is that there are plenty of viable business ideas all around you.

Infact, you know these ideas, you see them but haven't realized them yet or you haven't considered them to be good business ideas.

The world is full of opportunities if you know where to look. As Richard Branson once said, "Business opportunities are like buses, there's always another one coming."

In the upcoming discussion, I will guide you through various methods to uncover these ideas. I'll encourage you to be open-minded and generate as many ideas as possible.

Once you have a list, I'll introduce you to a helpful tool called the Clear Idea Matrix. This tool will assist you in organizing your ideas and preparing for the testing phase.

But before we begin, it's important to emphasize the fundamental principle that underlies every successful business.

The foundation of every remarkable business is solving a problem. Every entrepreneur has the innate ability to address the wants, needs, frustrations, and aspirations of others by offering a valuable solution.

The ultimate goal is to create a solution that leaves customers feeling satisfied, grateful, and willing. As we embark on this lesson to discover viable business ideas, it's crucial to remember the principle of problem-solving.

Like a friend of mine would often say;

"If your business idea is only to generate you money and not to solve a problem, then you don't have a business yet.

If you cannot clearly articulate how your business idea solves a specific problem, it may not be a viable concept that can thrive. So, always keep in mind that your idea must solve a problem.

Step 1: Generating Business Ideas

Get ready to unleash your creativity and start coming up with exciting business ideas using your planner. Set aside a specific timeframe, whether it's a week or a schedule that works best for you, dedicated to this important brainstorming process.

Use your planner to plan how much time you want to allocate for your "Business Idea Brainstorm." Remember, during this brainstorming session, there are no wrong or silly ideas.

I can list for you business ideas that seemed silly at first thought but became successful eventually.

There's Airbnb where initially, the concept of staying in a stranger's home seemed odd to many people. However, Airbnb disrupted the hotel industry and became a multi-billion-dollar company.

There's also a product called Poopouri which is a before-you-go toilet spray that helps eliminate unpleasant odors. The idea of a spray to cover up bathroom smells seemed unusual, but it gained popularity and became a successful business.

So, I implore you to give yourself permission to silence your inner critic and create a judgment-free environment.

The main goal here is to generate a significant number of ideas and enjoy the process. Don't worry about whether someone else has already pursued a similar business idea or if it's something you personally want to pursue.

Evaluating and making decisions will come later. Right now, focus on coming up with a minimum of 10 business ideas and embrace the journey.

If inspiration strikes and you come up with more than that, feel free to keep going. Just make sure you don't stop until you reach the minimum goal.

Setting a target of 10 ideas is important because it pushes you to expand your creative boundaries. By going slightly beyond your comfort zone—mentally, creatively, physically, emotionally, or spiritually—you open yourself up to new insights and unexpected connections.

Furthermore, as you progress to the stage of organizing and testing your business ideas for viability, you will naturally eliminate some of them.

This narrowing down process is crucial for maintaining focus. By starting with a larger quantity, you can gradually filter them down to a few select ideas with strong potential.

You may find that certain methods for idea generation resonate more with you than others, and that's perfectly fine. We have provided various approaches to ensure you have different tools at your disposal to generate at least 20 viable business ideas.

It's important to understand that the time required to complete this exercise may vary for different individuals. Your schedule and the speed of your thinking, creating, and executing will determine the duration.

Once you know where and how to find business ideas, your subconscious mind will continue working on them even when you're not consciously focused on the task.

Be prepared for unexpected moments of inspiration, whether they occur during your shower or commute. Whenever a new idea comes to mind, make sure to write it down in your planner and add it to your brainstorming list.

Now, let's explore four approaches that will spark your imagination and bring you closer to your goal of generating 20 or more viable business ideas while incorporating your planner into the process.

Approach #1: Solve Problems You Encounter

The story of Sara Blakely is an inspiring example of entrepreneurship and innovation. It all started with a simple but frustrating problem that many women face: uncomfortable and ill-fitting undergarments.

Sara, like many others, struggled to find undergarments that provided comfort and a smooth silhouette under clothing. Instead of accepting this as the norm, Sara decided to take matters into her own hands.

Without any formal background in fashion or business, she embarked on a mission to create a better solution.

In her apartment, she experimented with different fabrics and cuts, working tirelessly to perfect her invention. Her goal was to provide women with undergarments that were both comfortable and flattering, boosting their confidence and self-esteem.

Eventually, her hard work paid off, and she invented Spanx, a line of shapewear that revolutionized women's dressing experience.

However, Sara's journey didn't end there. She faced numerous challenges, including skepticism from experts in the industry and the difficulties of entering a competitive market. Nevertheless, she persisted and used her creativity and resourcefulness to overcome these obstacles.

Sara's determination and belief in her product led her to take bold steps, such as reaching out to influential individuals like Oprah Winfrey, who featured Spanx on her talk show. This exposure propelled the brand into the spotlight, leading to widespread success.

Sara Blakely's story is not only a testament to her entrepreneurial success but also an inspiration for aspiring business owners. It highlights the power of recognizing personal frustrations and finding innovative solutions.

By observing the problems, we encounter in our own lives, we can embark on an entrepreneurial path and make a meaningful impact.

After hearing Sara Blakely's story, it's time to apply her approach to your own life.

Take a moment to reflect on your daily activities and interactions.

Pay attention to both mundane tasks and conversations you have with others.

Are there recurring problems or frustrations that you wish had better solutions?

Are there areas of your life where you think, "I wish someone would come up with a better way to _____?"

These recurring problems hold potential for business ideas. Embrace the problem/solution framework and let your creativity flow. As part of your brainstorming process, challenge yourself to identify five problems for which you'd like to see new solutions.

These problems can serve as the foundation for potential business ideas. Don't worry about having all the answers or qualifications right now. The goal is to think outside the box and explore the possibilities.

Grab your planner, allocate time in your schedule for this exercise, and allow yourself the freedom to think creatively. Write down any recurring problems you encounter and their potential solutions.

Remember, this is just the beginning, and your ideas can evolve and be refined as you progress.

By following Sara Blakely's example and examining your own life, you have the opportunity to uncover unique business ideas that address real-world challenges.

Embrace the process, trust your instincts, and let your entrepreneurial journey begin.

If you are looking for the easiest and the most profitable online business for moms, click on this link to try out 30-Day Course Moremee.

DAY 3

How do you come up with ideas for your business (II)

Approach #2: Identify Your Strengths, Skills, and Interests

Each person possesses their own unique strengths, talents, and skills that set them apart. These qualities give you the ability to make a meaningful impact and provide solutions to the world.

By acknowledging your individual strengths, you open yourself up to discovering business ideas that align with your innate abilities.

To uncover these ideas, take a fresh perspective on your strengths, skills, and interests. Approach this exploration with curiosity as you delve into who you are and what comes naturally to you.

Consider how you can utilize your unique strengths, skills, gifts and I dare to say, even your weakness to solve problems for others.

Let me give you a list of entrepreneurs who mined their strength, skill and interest which in turn became what they sell today.

Oprah Winfrey leveraged her skills in communication and her interest in storytelling to create a media empire. She started as a television host and went on to establish OWN (Oprah Winfrey Network), Harpo Productions, and O, The Oprah Magazine.

Mark Zuckerberg who with a strong interest in computer programming and a knack for innovation, created Facebook while studying at Harvard University. His passion for connecting people and building social networks propelled him to become one of the most successful tech entrepreneurs.

Richard Branson's strength lies in his ability to identify gaps in the market and his adventurous spirit. He founded the Virgin Group, which started with Virgin Records and expanded into various industries such as aviation (Virgin Atlantic), mobile (Virgin Mobile), and space tourism (Virgin Galactic).

Bill Gates possessed exceptional programming skills and a deep interest in computers. Alongside Paul Allen, he co-founded Microsoft, which became one of the most influential software companies globally, dominating the personal computer operating system market.

And so on and so forth, these entrepreneurs are just a few examples of individuals who used their strengths, skills, and interests to launch successful businesses and products.

By leveraging their passions and expertise, they were able to make a significant impact in their respective industries. Recognizing your top strengths and skills may be challenging, but the following questions can help you identify your exceptional capabilities.

The goal is to unearth your inherent superpowers, so don't overthink or strive for perfection—simply jot down your initial responses.

If you could get paid to do or make something for others, what would it be?

What day-to-day tasks do you enjoy?

What gives you the most satisfaction at your current job?

What are you naturally good at or enjoy doing that others struggle with?

What have been your most enjoyable work experiences?

What skills do you have that could be translated into services?

What do people appreciate you doing for them?

What tools or online applications do you excel at using?

How do you spend your free time?

If money were no object, what would you do with your life?

What do people often ask for your help with?

Who do you admire professionally and why?

Whose job or business do you wish you had, and why?

What subjects do you read about?

What websites do you frequently visit?

What industries or fields do you follow?

What frustrates you about an industry, product, or service that you would like to change?

Which industries or revenue models excite you?

If you could start a business doing anything in the world, what would it be?

Remember, the goal is to uncover potential business ideas that stem from your unique strengths and skills.

Embrace the process with an open mind and let your genuine responses guide you.

This journey of discovery will lead you to valuable insights and the realization of your entrepreneurial potential.

Don't forget that all successful businesses are built around helping people solve problems.

 Review your responses and challenge yourself to identify at least five potential business ideas to add to your brainstorming list.

If you are looking for the easiest and the most profitable online business for moms, click on this link to try out 30-Day Course Moremee.

DAY 4

How do you come up with ideas for your business (III)

Approach #3: Seek Inspiration from Existing Businesses

Exploring businesses that align with your interests can spark ideas for your own potential ventures. Whether it's in design, education, fitness, pet care, healthcare, wellness, food, financial services, technology, or any other field that captures your attention, existing companies can serve as a great source of inspiration.

As you observe and analyze these businesses, pay attention to your inner voice. Notice which ideas resonate with you and evoke thoughts like,

"I would love to run a similar business,"

or "I've always wanted to pursue something like that,"

or "I believe I can offer a unique and improved approach to this."

Pay attention to physical cues as well, such as a sense of excitement, fear, or alignment that you may feel when encountering specific industries or business ideas. Trust these sensations as potential indicators of inspiration.

To start exploring ideas, utilize online resources. Websites like Inc.com, Entrepreneur Magazine, and Fast Company regularly feature diverse businesses and entrepreneurs, providing ample material to spark ideas.

Look for local publications relevant to your region as well, as entrepreneurship is a global phenomenon. Here are examples of entrepreneurs who used this approach to launch their own businesses.

The founders of Uber found inspiration in the traditional taxi industry. They aimed to create a more convenient and efficient transportation option by leveraging technology.

Uber's app-based platform revolutionized the ride-hailing industry and transformed the way people commute in many cities worldwide.

The founder of Alibaba, Jack Ma, drew inspiration from the success of established e-commerce companies like Amazon and eBay. He recognized the untapped potential of e-commerce in China and launched Alibaba, which rapidly grew to become one of the world's largest e-commerce conglomerates.

So, these entrepreneurs took inspiration from existing businesses or concepts and added their own innovative twists, ultimately creating successful ventures that disrupted industries and transformed the way we interact and conduct business.

Also engaging with entrepreneurial shows like Shark Tank and The Profit can also provide valuable insights and expose you to businesses across various industries.

If these shows aren't available, search for similar programs or resources in your area.

Google is a powerful tool for research. Simply searching for terms like "business ideas in design" or "business ideas in healthcare" will lead you to articles, blog posts, and resources to explore and inspire your ideation process.

Additionally, actively participate in business-oriented communities online and offline.

Join meetup groups, attend seminars, conferences, and networking events where you can connect with fellow business owners and immerse yourself in a sea of ideas and inspiration.

It's important to avoid deflating yourself by thinking that all the great ideas have already been taken. Remember, with over 7 billion people in the world, there is room for multiple players in any industry.

Many businesses address similar problems, and customers often support and engage with multiple vendors in the same industry. As you progress, think strategically about how you can differentiate yourself from competitors.

Consider carving out a unique niche, offering a distinctive value proposition, or providing an innovative twist within your chosen market.

Throughout this process, challenge yourself to add at least five more business ideas to your brainstorming list. Stay open-minded, remain inspired, and let your imagination flourish as you move closer to discovering the perfect business concept for you.

If you are looking for the easiest and the most profitable online business for moms, click on this link to try out 30-Day Course Moremee.

DAY 5

How do you come up with ideas for your business (IV)

Approach #4: Harnessing Creativity and Seeking Guidance

In the realm of idea mysticism, there are two methods that can help you find creative inspiration when you're feeling stuck. I call this method, generating ideas from thin air.

Embody Your Creativity:

Creativity is not just a mental process—it resides in your body too. Engaging in physical activities like exercise can spark remarkable ideas.

Research shows that activities like walking can significantly boost creative inspiration, with individuals experiencing a 60% increase in creative output while walking.

The specific form of exercise doesn't matter as much as simply getting active. Move your body, break a sweat, and if you enjoy it, listen to uplifting music while doing so. Ideas and breakthroughs often emerge naturally when you shift your focus to your body, embrace movement, and let music inspire you.

Practice: Engage in physical activity that resonates with you for at least 45 minutes, while listening to an energizing playlist. Whether it's dancing, running, cycling, or any other form of exercise, fully immerse yourself in the experience and remain open-minded. Repeat this practice daily.

Seek Guidance:

If you have faith in a higher power or the universe, reach out and seek assistance. Offer your prayers or intentions for help and be receptive to guidance.

It may come in unexpected ways, such as a brilliant idea striking you in an ordinary moment or through an invitation to a social gathering. Believe in the existence of a supportive life force that responds when you humbly seek its assistance and remain open to its answers.

I remember the story of a woman I was told. She got married and relocated to her spouse's area. Hence, she had to leave her job. For months she was home with nothing to do.

She was yet to get a job. She decided to seek guidance. She offered her prayer asking for what she could venture into.

She was then led to drive round the estate in which she lives with her husband. This she did and she was able to identify a no problem that needed solution in that estate.

It was the supply of drinkable water.

That was how she began her water supply business and today, she has many branches of her water company situated all over the country.

So it works.

Affirmation: I am ready and willing to receive the perfect business idea for me. I will take action while remaining open to guidance.

Remember, the goal is not to stress about generating a specific number of ideas. If you can't come up with the suggested number, trust yourself and move forward with the ideas you have.

You can always revisit and repeat the brainstorming process if needed. Progress is more important than perfection.

DAY 6

The Clear Idea Matrix - Reviewing and Organizing Business Ideas

Now that you have generated numerous ideas, it's time to review and organize them using a tool called The Clear Idea Matrix. This tool helps you analyze and make progress towards launching the perfect business for you.

Let's look at the first six fields of the matrix:

Business Idea: Give each idea a clear and simple name. It doesn't have to be overly creative or permanent, just distinguishable.

Examples: Coffee shop, Mobile app development, Event planning service, Eco-friendly cleaning products.

Problem: Summarize the problems each idea aims to solve in a few words.

Example for a coffee shop: Provides a cozy gathering place for community members to enjoy quality coffee and socialize.

Your Solution: Describe your solution to the problem and note any unique aspects.

Example for a coffee shop: We aim to create a welcoming space that offers high-quality coffee, fosters a sense of community, and stands out by sourcing organic beans, partnering with local artisans, and hosting live music performances.

Clear Revenue Model (Y/N): Indicate if you have a clear understanding of how this idea will generate revenue. Here you allocate what model will be used to generate income/revenue from each listed idea.

Will it be a direct sales model which involves selling products or services directly to customers?

Revenue is generated through one-time purchases or recurring subscriptions. Examples are retail stores, e-commerce, etc.

Will revenue generation from the idea be a subscription-based revenue model where customers pay a recurring fee to access a product or service over a specific period.

Examples include subscription boxes, streaming services, membership-based platforms, and software subscriptions.

Other revenue models includes Freemium which is a model which offers a basic version of a product or service for free while charging for additional features or premium versions. With this model companies entice customers with the free version and generate revenue through upselling.

Consulting or Professional Services where the businesses offer specialized knowledge, expertise, or professional services and charge clients based on the scope of work, hourly rates, or project fees. Examples include management consulting firms, law firms, marketing agencies, and freelancers.

So, these revenue models provide different approaches to generating income, and many businesses combine multiple models or adapt them to suit their specific industry or target market.

Competition (Y/N): Indicate if there are existing competitors in the marketplace for this idea. With this knowledge, you will be able to make some strategic decision. Remember, competition can indicate a viable market.

People You Will Serve/Target Audience: Provide a brief description of your ideal customers. Be specific and define your target market, considering their demographics, needs, and preferences.

Transfer all your ideas to The Clear Idea Matrix, regardless of the number. Pay attention to indicators like a lack of clear revenue model, no competition, difficulty articulating the problem, or lack of enthusiasm for the target customers. These may suggest ideas not worth pursuing.

The Clear Idea Matrix is a flexible framework for organizing your thoughts and analyzing your ideas. Customize it by adding or adjusting fields to suit your needs. The goal is to gain clarity and take smart, strategic, and consistent action.

After transferring your ideas to the matrix, the next step is to evaluate and test each idea, which we will guide you through in the following steps.

If you are looking for the easiest and the most profitable online business for moms, click on this link to try out 30-Day Course Moremee.

DAY 7

When You Can't Choose Among Multiple Passions (I)

Having multiple skills, talents, and interests can make it difficult to choose just one focus for your business. It's a common struggle, and I've experienced it myself as a multi-passionate entrepreneur.

I wanted to pursue various endeavors but felt torn about selecting just one. I sought guidance from experts who emphasized the importance of focus and specialization. While their advice made sense, I struggled with the idea of choosing a single focus. It felt like I was giving up a part of myself. I felt embarrassed when asked about my work because I didn't have a clear answer.

Eventually, I found a way to make peace with my multi-passionate nature and make progress in my business.

Here are the key elements that helped me:

Embracing a different approach: Instead of striving for conventional success, I allowed myself to think and act differently as a multi-passionate entrepreneur.

Valuing variety and flexibility: I accepted slower progress and potentially lower revenue in exchange for pursuing multiple passions concurrently.

Transitioning to a core focus: I decided to bring all my passions under one umbrella, serving a specific target audience. I made a deliberate choice to narrow down my focus while still doing everything I want

I'll share how these intentional shifts allowed me to embrace my multi-passionate nature and strategically determine which passions would receive more of my time and attention.

Please make sure you have listed all your potential passions as individual business ideas in your Clear Idea Matrix. As we go through this lesson, you may gain insights that help you eliminate certain ideas.

In the following sections, we will perform sanity checks, listen to our gut feelings, and explore a universal truth to evaluate our passions and create a customized action plan. If you have one single idea already, you can skip this part and proceed to the next steps:

Sanity Check #1: Not Every Passion Should Be Monetized

As a multi-passionate person, you may want to turn all your passions into business ventures. However, it's important to be cautious and consider whether monetizing every passion is the right choice.

Here are some reasons why it's beneficial to refrain from monetizing all your passions and maintain a balance: Not all passions are suitable for business: Some passions, like enjoying roller coasters, may not make practical business ideas. It's okay to enjoy certain passions personally without the pressure of making money from them.

Non-monetized passions boost creativity: Engaging in passions that aren't directly monetized can enhance your creativity and bring fresh ideas to your core business. Enjoying these passions purely for fun and inspiration creates space for innovation.

Personal fulfillment matters: Monetizing a passion doesn't always guarantee personal fulfillment. Some passions are better kept as hobbies or side interests to maintain a healthy balance. Prioritizing well-being and happiness lead to greater overall satisfaction.

Focus on what truly matters: Just because a passion can become a business doesn't mean it should. For example, someone who excels in team management but is also passionate about interior design may choose to focus on their expertise rather than starting a design firm. It's about finding fulfillment in your existing field.

As you navigate your multi-passionate journey, resist the urge to monetize every passion. Some passions are best enjoyed personally for pure joy and inspiration. Reassess your list and eliminate ideas that are impractical for starting a business or that you don't genuinely want to pursue as a means of making a living.

Remember, having enthusiasm or skills in an area doesn't automatically mean starting a business around it.

If you are looking for the easiest and the most profitable online business for moms, click on this link to try out 30-Day Course Moremee.

DAY 8

When You Can't Choose Among Multiple Passions (II)

Sanity Check #2: Adjusting Your Lifestyle to Embrace Your Passions

When I started my entrepreneurial journey, I had numerous passions and goals I wanted to pursue professionally. However, my life circumstances presented challenges, such as having young children, financial setbacks, and limited support.

Despite these obstacles, I chose to prioritize my long-term goals and stay focused. You might be in a different life stage with a full-time job, family commitments, financial obligations, and various responsibilities. But this doesn't mean you can't embrace your multi-passionate nature and start the right business.

It just requires strategic thinking, resourcefulness, and responsible choices. Instead of pursuing all your passions simultaneously to determine which one is best for a long-term business focus, consider dedicating specific hours each week to testing one passion at a time.

This might mean adjusting your schedule, having honest conversations with loved ones, or making lifestyle changes to create more time and financial freedom.

For example, let's say you have five passions and you're torn between two for your business. Allocate eight weeks to individually test each idea. By dedicating two hours a day, five days a week, to Passion #1 for one month, you'll have invested a total of 40 hours.

Evaluate the results, document your insights, and then test Passion #2 for the next four weeks. No matter the outcome, you'll be ahead and have personal data and experiences to guide your next steps.

To find the necessary time, minimize media consumption, manage email effectively, delegate household chores, and adjust your sleep schedule if needed.

While progress may be slower than expected, it's important to be okay with that. Don't obsess over speed or time constraints. Embrace your current life stage, make adjustments, and take deliberate steps forward.

Remember, the journey is just as important as the destination, and your progress will come through consistent action

If you are looking for the easiest and the most profitable online business for moms, click on this link to try out 30-Day Course Moremee.

DAY 9

When You Can't Choose Among Multiple Passions (III)

Sanity Check #3: Identify Your Life Goals and Explore Future Scenarios

When pursuing a multi-passionate path, it's important to align your business endeavors with your overall life goals. This involves gaining clarity about your next important life goals and exploring different future possibilities that match your aspirations.

Start by reflecting on your life and identifying your significant milestones or objectives. These can be personal, professional, or lifestyle-related. For example, you might want financial stability, more time with family, travel experiences, societal impact, or personal growth. Knowing your life goals will guide your decisions as a multi-passionate entrepreneur.

Next, visualize different future scenarios that align with your passions and interests. Imagine yourself engaged in various business ventures or professional paths that allow you to achieve your goals.

For me, I picture myself as a successful product manager, consultant, online store owner, or course creator.

Now picture yourself in the future you want

While doing this, take note of your excitement and sense of fulfillment in each scenario.

How did you feel when you pictured yourself to be in scenario one?

What you felt when you imagined yourself to be in scenario two?

So for each of this scenarios you must carefully take note of the feeling you had.

To gain a deeper understanding of these potential futures, try out different roles or opportunities. Take up part-time positions, freelance, volunteer, or shadow professionals in your desired fields.

Immersing yourself in these experiences will provide valuable insights into the practicalities, challenges, and rewards associated with each role.

Continuously assess the alignment between your explored paths and life goals. Determine if each potential future supports your desired lifestyle, helps you make progress toward your personal objectives, and brings you joy and fulfillment.

Then prioritize opportunities that resonate deeply with your overarching vision. Throughout this process of exploration and self-reflection, be open to refining your focus.

At this point, you adjust your direction and discard ideas that no longer serve your larger purpose. The goal is to create a cohesive and sustainable multi-passionate business that brings you long-term satisfaction and supports your desired lifestyle.

Remember, knowing your life goals and exploring future scenarios is an important sanity check to ensure your multi-passionate pursuits align with your aspirations.

Evaluate each opportunity consciously to build a business that integrates your passions, fulfills your life goals, and provides a sense of purpose and fulfillment.

ACTION STEPS:

Consider your next major life goals and how you want to spend your time and earn money. Envision different future scenarios in the businesses or industries you're considering.

Evaluate your willingness to put in the effort and whether it excites you. Cross off passions that don't align with your goals, but remember they can still be part of your life. Prioritize what resonates most and embrace the path that brings fulfillment.

If you are looking for the easiest and the most profitable online business for moms, click on this link to try out 30-Day Course Moremee.

DAY 10

Gut Check: The Test for the Next 10 Years

Sometimes, trusting your instincts is valuable when choosing an idea or pursuing a new venture. The "10 Years Test" is a helpful way to evaluate an idea.

Here's how it works:

Imagine yourself ten years from now, looking back on the decision you're about to make. Ask yourself if you will regret not pursuing this idea or opportunity.

Think about the potential outcomes, both positive and negative, that may come from following this path. Picture your future self reflecting on the choices you made. Pay attention to the emotions you feel as you imagine this scenario.

If imagining your future self leaves you with a deep sense of regret or a feeling that you missed out on something important, it suggests that this idea is worth exploring further. Your intuition is giving you valuable insight into the significance and impact of this decision.

On the other hand, if you feel indifferent or unenthusiastic about the idea when considering your future self, it may not align with your long-term aspirations and values.

Remember, the 10 Years Test is not foolproof, but it can help you gain clarity and make decisions that align with your inner desires and aspirations. Trusting your instincts often leads to fulfillment and satisfaction in the long run.

Take a moment to imagine yourself ten years from now, evaluate your ideas using the 10 Years Test, and listen to your intuition as you choose the path that resonates most with your future self.

ACTION STEP: Evaluate your remaining passions using the 10-Year Test, focusing on their potentials as a business endeavor. Ask yourself, "Will I regret not pursuing this passion as a business ten years from now?"

Remember, the key here is to consider whether you want to transform the passion into a viable business venture. You might find that you'll regret not devoting more time and energy to a specific passion, which provides valuable insight.

However, it's important to differentiate between wanting to explore a passion and being fully committed to turning it into a business. Only you can honestly answer this question. Starting a business is challenging, so you're looking for a strong, instinctive response to this inquiry.

After applying the 10-Year Test to each remaining passion, revisit your list of business ideas and eliminate any passion that doesn't elicit a strong enough commitment from you.

Focus on the passions that you feel compelled to dedicate the majority of your time, energy, and life to for the next 2-5 years. A lukewarm response rarely leads to a useful outcome.

Remember, if it's not a resounding "hell yes," then it's a definite "hell no." Trust your gut and prioritize the passions that ignite your inner fire and align with your long-term goals.

If you are looking for the easiest and the most profitable online business for moms, click on this link to try out 30-Day Course Moremee.

DAY 11

How Do You Know If Your Idea Will Make You Money?

Determining if your idea will make you money can be challenging, but it's important to focus on the right things and avoid common pitfalls.

Many entrepreneurs get caught up in minor details like business structure or branding before knowing if their product will sell, but these details aren't crucial at this stage.

It's also important to seek feedback from the right people. Don't rely solely on friends who may offer generic encouragement. Instead, consult individuals with experience and success in your desired field who share your values and understand your goals. You could even get a coach.

To accurately gauge commercial viability, don't just ask people if they would buy your product; ask them to actually make a purchase. Their response to this question is what truly matters.

Also, offering your product or service for free or at a discounted rate in the early stages can provide valuable feedback and help you improve your offering.

It's also important to focus on getting actual sales. Mere expressions of interest are not enough; people need to be willing to pay for what you offer for your business to succeed or else, your business might run at loss.

By following these steps, you can choose a business idea, understand your customers' needs and the competition, make offers, and use customer feedback to improve and build trust.

If you are looking for the easiest and the most profitable online business for moms, click on this link to try out 30-Day Course Moremee.

DAY 12

The Common Sense Test (I)

Before we continue, we need to go through a test called "The Common Sense Test." It consists of four simple but important questions.

This test will help you objectively evaluate the ideas in your Clear Idea Matrix. By eliminating ideas that don't meet the criteria, you can confidently choose one idea to move forward with.

The main goal of this lesson is to select a single business idea from your Clear Idea Matrix.

Here's how The Common Sense Test works: If you can't answer "yes" to all four questions below, it's best to remove that idea from your list.

Are you ready? Let's get started!

Question #1: Do I have the right experience, skills, or abilities for this product or service? If not, am I ready to fully commit to learning and acquiring them?

A Yes or a No?

This question is easy to understand, and the answer should be very clear.

If you want to create a physical product, do you already know how to do it?

If not, are you willing to spend time and effort on researching and learning the necessary steps?

Remember, with the right mindset, you can figure out anything. But if you're not truly dedicated to taking the necessary steps to make your idea a reality, it's best to let go of that idea.

For example, if you want to start a personal training business but you don't have a fitness routine, the motivation, or the determination to become a certified personal trainer, it's wise to abandon that business idea.

Similarly, if you want to be a small business coach or an online marketing coach, it's important to have firsthand experience in running a successful small business or a proven track record of successful online marketing.

Simply reading books, listening to podcasts, or taking courses from others is not enough. Every small business has the potential to make a meaningful impact, but it must be built on a foundation of honesty, integrity, and transparency.

If you currently lack the necessary experience, skills, or abilities but you're genuinely willing to put in the necessary work to acquire them, then it's time to take action. However, it's crucial to not pretend to be something you're not.

Remember, if your answer to this first question is "no," it's best to let go of that idea. If your answer is "yes," then let's move on to the next step.

If you are looking for the easiest and the most profitable online business for moms, click on this link to try out 30-Day Course Moremee.

DAY 13

The Common Sense Test (II)

Question #2: Are you ready to commit the majority of your free time to this endeavor for at least the next year?

Do you have a strong passion, enthusiasm, and a desire to solve problems for your target market? Starting a business solely for money is unlikely to succeed in the long run. My coach would always say

"Create ideas because you want to solve problems not just because you want to make money."

It's important to be genuinely obsessed with the problem you're solving, the solution you're offering, or the people you're serving.

Now, let's talk about the "majority of your free time" aspect.

Many entrepreneurs start their businesses while working full-time or having other commitments. It's challenging to balance these demands, but if you're truly dedicated to your business idea, it's worth the effort.

When I started my own business, I worked tirelessly, sacrificing TV and social activities.

I woke up early, stayed up late, and put my social life on hold.

If you genuinely care about your business, you'll find ways to make time for it, even if you have other responsibilities.

Busy people often manage their time effectively because they have to.

Countless small business owners with various limitations and constraints find time to work on their ideas.

So, ask yourself if you're willing to devote the majority of your free time to your business for the next year. Are you ready to give up TV, mindless scrolling on social media, and non-essential activities?

Regardless of your circumstances, you must consistently make time to grow your business.

Lastly, let's address the "next 12 months" part.

We can't predict how quickly your business will succeed. It may take months or even years before you see stable and profitable growth.

The 12-month timeframe allows for testing, feedback, and long-term commitment.

If you're genuinely excited, a year will feel short, but if you lack enthusiasm, it will feel like a burden.

In summary, if you're passionate, willing to commit time and energy, and ready for a long-term commitment, then you're prepared to dedicate the majority of your free time to your business for the next year.

If you are looking for the easiest and the most profitable online business for moms, click on this link to try out 30-Day Course Moremee.

DAY 14

The Common Sense Test (III)

Question #3: Does this idea align with my goal of building a micro, small, or large-scale business?

It's important to make sure your business idea matches your goals for the size of your business and the kind of life you want.

For example, if you want to have a bakery in your neighborhood but also want to travel a lot and work from anywhere, those two goals might not fit together well.

Running a bakery usually requires your daily presence and attention, which could conflict with your desire for a location-independent lifestyle.

While it's possible to eventually delegate tasks and have more freedom, it might take time to get there and delay your desired lifestyle in the short term.

Consider your desired lifestyle, current responsibilities, and how much time and effort your business idea will demand.

Starting and running any business requires a lot of focus, hard work, and commitment.

Remember that every business, no matter its size, has its own challenges and obstacles that need to be overcome.

Make sure your chosen business idea matches your dream business in terms of scale and what you want to achieve.

If it doesn't match, it's important to remove it from your list and look for alternatives that are better fits for your goals.

If you are looking for the easiest and the most profitable online business for moms, click on this link to try out 30-Day Course Moremee.

DAY 15

The Common Sense Test (IV)

Question 4: Is there a clear and easy-to-reach group of people who are already buying this type of product or service?

This is an important question to consider when starting a business, as it affects the financial viability of your idea.

To increase your chances of success and minimize frustration, it's advisable to choose a market that already exists and is actively spending money on your proposed product or service.

Let me give you an example to illustrate this point:

Imagine you want to start a business coaching homeless men to help them get back on their feet.

While this group represents a specific market and can be reached through local shelters or support centers, homeless men typically don't have the means to spend money on life coaching services.

While you could offer your coaching for free or seek sponsorship, it may not be a viable target market for a for-profit business.

On the other hand, let's say you're a copywriter planning to start a business that provides persuasive content for beauty companies' websites, content marketing, and social media campaigns.

Beauty company owners make up a clearly defined market that actively invests money to grow their businesses. In this case, your idea would be more feasible.

Instead of developing a product or service and then looking for potential customers, follow these steps:

Identify a group of people you genuinely care about and can easily identify and reach.

Confirm that they are already spending money on the type of product or service you offer.

Engage with them, ask questions, and gain a deep understanding of their problems, frustrations, aspirations, and desires related to your offering.

Create a product or service that provides a solution they are willing to pay for and promote it effectively.

Being a member of your target market can be advantageous, as you have insights into their needs, frustrations, dreams, and spending habits.

If you belong to your target market, you likely have friends and acquaintances who can provide feedback or try your products or services.

Additionally, you may be aware of their preferred online and offline communities, such as newsletters, blogs, magazines, social media accounts, and podcasts they follow.

If you are not already a part of the group you want to sell to or unsure if people will be interested in your product or service idea, you can do thorough research.

Nowadays, it's easier than ever to conduct research because of how connected we are.

If you are looking for the easiest and the most profitable online business for moms, click on this link to try out 30-Day Course Moremee.

DAY 16

How to Make Research

Blogs: Find popular blogs in your category or topic to learn about what your target audience is worried about, what frustrates them, what they desire, and who the important people in the industry are.

Amazon: Look at relevant products and books, paying attention to the best reviews and sales rankings. This can give you an idea of how interested people are in the market.

Podcasts: Search for podcasts that are related to your industry or topic. By listening to them, you can discover experts, leaders in the field, and other similar offerings.

Social Media Groups: Join Facebook or LinkedIn groups that are relevant to your field. This will help you connect with individuals who are interested in what you have to offer.

Magazines: Visit bookstores that sell magazines focused on specific interests. This will give you insights into your industry through things like advertising rates and the number of readers.

Meetups: Look for local meetups that are focused on specific interests or communities that are related to your target market. This can help you connect with potential customers and learn more about their needs and preferences.

When you do research online, remember not to let yourself become overwhelmed. Remember that your goal is to find out if there is a specific group of people who are already buying the type of product or service you want to offer, and if they are easy to reach.

If you still feel unsure even after doing research, it might be a sign that you need to investigate further or think about different ideas that have a clearer and more accessible market.

Action Step: If you haven't done so already, review each item in your Clear Idea Matrix using the Common Sense Test.

Answer the four questions honestly and thoroughly.

The goal is to choose the right business venture for yourself.

If you find that your best business idea conflicts with your lifestyle goals, you have two options: adjust your lifestyle goals or look for a different business opportunity.

Keep it simple and clear.

Here are the four questions of the Common Sense Test again:

Do I have the knowledge, skills, or abilities needed for this product or service, or am I willing to put in a lot of effort to learn and develop them?

Am I ready to dedicate most of my free time to this idea for at least the next year?

Does this idea match my goal of starting a small, medium, or large business?

Is there a specific and easy-to-reach group of people who are already spending money on this particular product or service?

After applying these questions to each idea, choose ONE idea to proceed with in the next step.

If you have multiple good ideas, trust your intuition, logical thinking, and instincts to make a decision.

Take time to think, reflect, write in a journal, or do any activity that helps you make a clear and committed choice, focusing on a single idea. Understood?

Great! Now that you have ONE idea, you're ready to move forward to the next phase.

If you are looking for the easiest and the most profitable online business for moms, click on this link to try out 30-Day Course Moremee.

DAY 17

The Dollar & Sense Test

It's time to assess if your idea will attract your target audience. To do this, you need to complete The Dollars & Sense Test, which I'll explain in detail shortly.

The outcome is simple: by the end, you'll either have beta customers, paying customers, or be well on your way to acquiring them. But before we proceed, I need to share something important with you.

If, after sincerely completing The Dollars & Sense Test, you find out that this idea won't work, don't let it discourage you.

While that's not what we hope for, it's important to understand that every business owner faces significant challenges on the path to success.

We all experience setbacks, failures, and obstacles along our entrepreneurial journey. Some ideas succeed, while many do not.

The truth is that not every idea, product, or service takes off, no matter how intelligent, determined, or focused we are. But here's the key:

A setback isn't the end unless you choose to stay down.

If your initial idea doesn't work out, don't let it define your entire entrepreneurial potential.

Don't develop a limiting belief that you're not cut out to be an entrepreneur or that you lack the intelligence, capability, or worthiness to make things happen.

Yes, objectively analyze what went wrong. Be curious and identify areas where you may have overlooked crucial information or made inaccurate assumptions about your product or the market.

Learn from those lessons!

Then, as soon as possible, get back in the game, ask yourself,

"What do I need to do now to turn this around?

What actions should I take to keep moving forward?

How can I use my creativity, resourcefulness, and curiosity to make a more compelling offer or improve upon my previous attempts?"

From a practical standpoint, you can either refine your original idea based on the insights and experiences you've gained, persist and continue, or explore another idea and repeat this process.

As you know, nothing in business or life is guaranteed. The majority of new business owners don't get everything right on their first try.

However, be assured that following these steps will give you the best possible chance for success and ongoing growth.

 In business, perseverance matters more than tactics.

Don't give up!

Now, let's delve into The Dollars & Sense Test. As the name suggests, this test ensures that your business idea is financially viable and makes sense. We've divided it into three parts: customer research, industry expert research, and making offers

If you are looking for the easiest and the most profitable online business for moms, click on this link to try out 30-Day Course Moremee.

DAY 18

Conducting Customer Research

Customer research is about having real conversations with people. It's best to focus on a market you already have a connection with, whether socially, professionally, or recreationally. This shared ground makes it easier to talk to people and establish a connection.

If you don't have a prior connection to your target market, that's okay. Building rapport with strangers is an important skill for any successful business owner.

At this stage, your goal is not to sell anything. Instead, focus on connecting with others and asking questions that encourage them to talk about themselves, not about you.

People generally enjoy talking about themselves, and by engaging in conversation-based customer research, you are giving them the opportunity to be heard.

Questions are the powerful tool you'll use in this step. They will provide valuable insights about your market that you couldn't uncover on your own. You'll ask questions to learn:

The specific problems, frustrations, and challenges they face daily related to your product or service.

What currently works for them with the products or services they use (if applicable).

What doesn't work about their current solution? In other words, what could be improved?

The exact words they use to describe their problems and desired outcomes.

Instead of spending excessive time on complex packages, pricing structures, or preparing to launch your website, customer research will help you make progress more effectively.

Don't overthink or make the process too serious.

Whether you connect with potential customers online or offline, remember to manage your energy and approach the conversations with an open, warm, and service-oriented mindset.

Build genuine rapport by smiling, giving sincere compliments, or asking simple questions. Introduce yourself and let the conversation flow.

It's important to note that even through phone, email, or text, your emotions and energy are transmitted, so leverage that to your advantage.

For example, if you want to start a dog care business and you meet other dog owners during your daily dog walk, you can start a conversation by saying something like, "Your dog is beautiful. Is it a boy or a girl? By the way, I'm Tina. I'm working on an idea for a dog care business, and I'd love to get your opinion on..."

Quick tip: Asking for people's opinions is important. We all like to feel important and that our ideas matter.

Of course, not everyone may be interested in talking to you, and that's okay.

Rejection, skepticism, and hearing "no" are part of the entrepreneurial journey.

While I'm not suggesting you follow my dialogue as a word-for-word script, the idea is to start simple, casual conversations.

Continuing with the dog care business example, another step you can take is making a list of people you know who have dogs. Then, call them and ask about their current dog care situation. Ask them what's working and, most importantly, what's not working.

Don't forget to ask for referrals. Every dog owner you talk to should be asked to connect you with other dog owner friends you can talk to. This way, you'll quickly accumulate valuable customer research and potential future customers.

Now, let's explore some sample customer research questions to inspire you. Remember, this list is not exhaustive, and not every question will be relevant to your business.

Choose what's most applicable and use these prompts to create your own questions as well.

The goal is not to follow a strict customer research formula, but to become skilled at asking questions that genuinely help you understand your customers' needs, frustrations, and desires.

Action Steps: Take the following steps to achieve your goal of having meaningful conversations with 20 individuals who are part of your target market.

Aim to connect with 20 people who are aligned with your target market as quickly as possible, rather than prolonging this step for months.

Challenge yourself to complete this task within a few days.

When engaging in these conversations, give your full attention and focus to the person you are talking to.

If you're conversing in person, put your phone on silent mode and eliminate any potential distractions.

Be completely present in the moment during the conversation.

If appropriate, take notes to accurately record the exact words and phrases used by individuals when discussing their problems, frustrations, and desired solutions.

These specific words and phrases will be valuable resources for creating compelling content for your website and marketing materials.

If you are looking for the easiest and the most profitable online business for moms, click on this link to try out 30-Day Course Moremee.

DAY 19

Conducting Industry Expert Research

To gain valuable insights into your industry, it's crucial to connect with experts and peers who are already involved in the field.

Try to have conversations with at least five industry experts, and if possible, challenge yourself to engage with even more.

Why is this step so important?

Well, as Tony Robbins wisely said, "Success leaves clues." There are individuals who have already achieved what you aspire to accomplish or have similar experiences.

They possess extensive knowledge, insights into market trends, and valuable lessons that would otherwise take you years to learn on your own.

Before you dismiss the idea due to fear, shyness, or uncertainty about approaching industry experts, consider this perspective:

If you struggle to motivate yourself to connect with just five individuals in your desired industry, how do you expect to establish and manage a successful business within that industry?

I'm not saying this to be harsh, but rather to emphasize the level of determination, resourcefulness, and drive required to launch and sustain a business.

It involves putting yourself out there, building connections, and fostering relationships with both clients and colleagues.

First, think about the people you would love to connect with in your industry.

Write down their names, even if they are well-known or considered industry celebrities.

While it might be challenging to reach them directly, it's still worth including their names as unexpected opportunities can arise. Putting your thoughts on paper has a powerful effect on your subconscious mind and can lead to unexpected outcomes.

If you can't connect with prominent figures directly, you can still gain valuable insights from their in-depth interviews in books, documentaries, or podcasts. These resources offer a wealth of knowledge.

Consider the up-and-coming individuals in your field, as they are often more accessible and easier to connect with. Their advice and experiences may be more relatable to your current stage of the journey.

Think about individuals who were once in the spotlight but have since scaled back. They have valuable experience to share and are usually more approachable.

Don't hesitate to seek introductions from friends, family, and colleagues. They might know someone in your industry or field that could help you.

Networking through connections can lead to unexpected opportunities.

Make sure to write down the names of every person you can think of on your list.

When it comes to building relationships, it's important to be thoughtful and considerate. Try to understand the other person's life, priorities, and the best way to approach them.

Also, think about how you can make the relationship mutually beneficial.

Here are three approaches to consider, but remember to be creative and think outside the box when brainstorming ways to connect with someone:

Become a customer: If the person you want to connect with offers a product or service, consider engaging with their brand. Attend their talks, workshops, or courses, or become a customer of their products. This firsthand experience will help you understand who they are and what they offer.

For example, I wanted to be close to Julietta Raoul, the founder of Jullz creation, then I became her customer. The two hours spent with her were one of the best in a long time. No regret spending premium to meet her.

Afterward, send them a heartfelt letter expressing how their product or service positively impacted you. Business owners appreciate thoughtful notes from satisfied customers, and it can lead to further connection.

Write an article about them for a publication: Reach out to the expert and propose writing an article about them.

You can create a profile piece highlighting their achievements or include their insights as an expert in a larger industry-related article.

For example, you could write an article titled "7 Experts Predict What's Next in Mobile Marketing" and include their insights.

After editing the article for clarity, publish it and share it with the expert.

Make a direct connection: When approaching someone directly, be thoughtful and create a meaningful context that offers a win-win situation.

If you have a mutual acquaintance or friend, consider asking for an introduction. Find common ground, such as being from the same town or sharing interests, to initiate a conversation.

Another approach is to leverage recent events in their life, such as a new puppy, by suggesting relevant resources or offering friendly advice.

If you are already a customer and have benefited from their work, write a concise email or letter sharing a specific result or personal story related to the benefit you derived from their offerings.

When reaching out to busy people, keep your communication brief, heartfelt, and to the point.

Double-check your message for any spelling errors, and be kind and inclusive of their team.

Give them an easy way to decline, expressing gratitude for their work even if they are unable to respond.

If someone is willing to meet in person or over the phone, make the conversation about them by actively listening and asking questions about their journey and experiences.

Aim for the majority of the conversation to revolve around their insights and growth in the industry, and only share more about yourself toward the end.

Before concluding the conversation, present your business idea and seek their recommendations on starting off in the right direction. Show that you have done your homework and ask if they have any specific suggestions.

Finally, send a personal thank-you note after each meeting to express your appreciation

Here are simplified guidelines for building industry relationships:

Keep taking action to move your business forward while also focusing on building relationships with experts and colleagues. Don't stop or delay your progress.

Developing genuine relationships requires time and effort, so don't rush or try to force a connection.

Understand that the effort you put in now will bring long-term rewards. Your industry colleagues can offer valuable ideas, resources, and solutions when you face challenges in your business.

Be consistent, patient, and persistent in building these relationships. The benefits will be worth it.

Take the following action steps:

Set a goal to connect with and interview at least five individuals who have achieved success in the industry you want to work in.

These conversations will provide you with valuable insights that would otherwise take a long time to learn on your own. Be prepared for the possibility of rejection or being ignored.

Remember, it's not personal, and it should not discourage you. Persistence is crucial in business, and building relationships takes time.

Once you have completed your initial goal of five interviews, don't stop there. Continue expanding your network of industry colleagues.

Building these connections over time is a valuable asset that will benefit you throughout your career.

If you are looking for the easiest and the most profitable online business for moms, click on this link to try out 30-Day Course Moremee.

DAY 20

Making Offers (I)

Now that you have a deep understanding of your target market, competition, and future insights, it's time to put your knowledge into action by making offers.

Depending on whether you have a service-based or product-based business, there are two primary approaches: direct sales and collaboration opportunities. Let's look at each approach in detail.

Direct Sales: This strategy involves reaching out directly to potential customers and making offers to them. The goal is to introduce yourself, demonstrate the value you can provide, and gauge their interest in your product or service.

Here's an example to illustrate this approach:

Subject: Exciting Fitness Program Offer for [Prospective Client's Name]

Dear [Prospective Client's Name],

I recently discovered your work and was truly impressed by your commitment to helping people achieve their fitness goals. As a fellow fitness enthusiast, I greatly admire the impact you're making in the industry.

I'm reaching out today because I have developed a unique fitness program that aligns perfectly with your mission. It combines high-intensity interval training, functional movements, and personalized nutrition plans to deliver exceptional results.

To showcase the effectiveness of my program, I would like to offer you a complimentary one-month membership. During this time, you'll have access to personalized training sessions, nutritional guidance, and ongoing support from me as your personal trainer.

I understand your time is valuable, and I want to assure you that my program is designed to deliver tangible results. If you find value in the program and experience its impact on your fitness journey, I would be thrilled to discuss further collaboration possibilities, such as becoming your dedicated personal trainer or exploring joint ventures.

You can find more details about my program and testimonials from satisfied clients on my website at [website URL]. I genuinely believe that this opportunity will not only benefit you personally but also enhance your ability to inspire and transform the lives of others through your platform.

I would love to connect with you and discuss how we can work together to empower individuals to reach their fitness goals. Please feel free to reach out to me at [contact information] or simply respond to this email. Thank you for your time and consideration.

Best regards, [Your Name]

This example demonstrates how approaching someone directly and offering a complimentary service or product can capture their attention and potentially lead to a valuable business relationship.

By showcasing the value of your offer and aligning it with their goals or mission, you increase the chances of them being interested in exploring further collaboration.

Remember to be persistent in direct sales. If you don't receive a response, don't take it personally. Instead, continue refining your approach, adjusting your pitches, and seeking feedback to improve your chances of success.

Create a comprehensive list of at least 30 people or businesses that you want to work with. Spend at least two hours each day crafting personalized emails and sending them to your prospects.

As you make progress, continue adding names to your list to increase your opportunities.

In the business world, numbers are important. There is a simple but powerful saying:

"The more you make, the more you make."

This means that the more offers you extend, the more sales you are likely to generate.

Think about this: If you only reach out to three people each day, you limit your potential achievements and slow down your progress.

But what if you committed to doubling, tripling, or even increasing your daily offers tenfold?

Undoubtedly, you would achieve greater and faster results. You would have the chance to impact more lives and improve your sales skills along the way.

Approach this process with an open mind and a receptive attitude.

Pay close attention to the feedback you receive.

Adapt and refine your email subject lines, offer content, and pitching technique until you find what resonates most effectively.

If you are looking for the easiest and the most profitable online business for moms, click on this link to try out 30-Day Course Moremee.

DAY 21

Making Offers (II)

Now, let's explore the second method of making offers.

Collaboration Opportunities: Within every business or industry, there are individuals or organizations that cater to the same target market without being direct competitors.

For example, in the fitness industry, people looking for personal trainers may also be interested in hiring a nutritionist or a massage therapist.

Similarly, in the film and photography industry, clients hiring photographers often need makeup artists, hair stylists, and clothing stylists.

Identify successful businesses that are already serving your desired target market, and propose providing your products or services to their customers.

Offering your products or services for free or at a discounted rate can greatly increase your chances of securing partnerships with potential collaborators.

Additionally, give your prospective partners the opportunity to experience your offerings firsthand, so they can see the professionalism and value you bring to their clients.

This approach shows your genuine desire for long-term relationships and partnerships within your industry, emphasizing generosity and authenticity.

As your own business grows, return the support by referring your clients or customers to your preferred partners. There are many partnership opportunities available if you think creatively and actively seek ways to help your partners succeed in the eyes of their customers.

ACTION STEPS: Think about the existing businesses that serve your target market.

How can you enhance the image of your potential partners by offering them a free or discounted product or service? How can you provide additional value to the partner and their audience?

Initiate contact and build genuine relationships with them. This approach requires time and effort, but securing just one or two key partners can significantly accelerate your growth.

Create a list of at least 5 potential partners, including their names, contact information, and potential offerings for them or their clients/customers.

Reach out to these potential partners using your list.

Remember that this is a numbers game, so be persistent in a positive and pleasant manner, and you will eventually succeed.

If you are looking for the easiest and the most profitable online business for moms, click on this link to try out 30-Day Course Moremee.

DAY 22

You're almost there!

Now you have everything you need to bring your idea to life!

The key is to check if people are really interested in what you have to offer.

So, go out and gather feedback from potential customers. Listen to what they say and make changes based on their input. Once you have a solid idea, it's time to explore further.

Take a closer look at your target market and examine the competition. Do some research on the market, build relationships, and get to know others in your industry.

The goal is to understand the business environment and find your place in it. Now comes the exciting part.

Start making offers! You can directly approach customers and explain how you can help them.

Alternatively, you can collaborate with businesses that already serve your target market. Offer your products or services for free or at a discounted price, and demonstrate your capabilities.

By doing this, you not only gain valuable experience but also make your potential partners look good to their clients.

As your idea gains momentum, it's important to refine your business model. Create a basic version of your product and establish an online presence.

Continuously improve and be open to feedback from customers. This iterative process will help you enhance your offering and make it even better.

Remember, entrepreneurship is not a solitary journey. Seek out mentors who can guide you, join entrepreneurial communities to connect with like-minded individuals, and attend industry events to learn and grow.

Surrounding yourself with supportive and inspiring people will make the journey much more enjoyable.

So, there you have it!

The key is to validate your idea, understand your market, make offers, and continually improve.

Get out there, connect with potential customers, and let your idea shine.

If you are looking for the easiest and the most profitable online business for moms, click on this link to try out 30-Day Course Moremee.

BONUS

Moremee's 24-Hour Quick Validation

My Journey of Success Empowered by Moms

I had a great idea that moms could join together and buy things at a lower cost. I believe that when moms come together, they can get discounts, support each other, and find new opportunities. That's how I came up with the idea for Moremee.

I was really excited and knew that I needed to prove that Moremee could work. So, I spent 24 hours working hard to show that it was a good idea.

First, I needed to find the perfect name for my platform. After thinking for a long time, I came up with Moremee. It represented moms coming together for more value and empowerment.

Once I had the name, I focused on creating a message that would get moms interested. I sent a WhatsApp message explaining the benefits of group buying and the support of a community. I wanted moms to feel excited about Moremee.

To bring Moremee to life, I created a WhatsApp group where moms could come together and discuss their group buying experiences. I also made a simple form to collect important information from interested moms.

I shared the Moremee WhatsApp group and form with moms in a community where I was already active. I wanted to reach moms who were open to new opportunities and collective buying.

Amazingly, moms from different backgrounds joined Moremee. In just a few hours, we had 26 enthusiastic members. It was clear that moms liked the idea of group buying.

The momentum kept growing. The word spread quickly, and we had 52 members the next day. What surprised me the most was that 70% of moms who joined our group actually made purchases. They were not just interested; they actively took part and benefited from our collective power.

In just 24 hours, I learned some important lessons. I realized that taking quick action, creating messages that connect with moms, and using existing networks are important for validation.

The fast validation of Moremee motivated me to keep going and make it even better. I believe in the power of having a vision, being determined, and having the support of moms working together.

As I continue with Moremee, I look forward to a future where moms everywhere can experience the joy of collective buying power, build strong connections, and feel empowered.

This is my story—a story of Moremee's quick validation and the exciting possibilities that lie ahead.

SPEAK TO US

My companies, Moremee and Rapid Launch, offers corporate team training and consultation around the topics of Product Management, Idea Generation & Validation, and Innovation workshops. If you'd like to ask us something or get us to visit your company, just email rafiat@moremee.co and we'll get right back to you!

If you are looking for the easiest and the most profitable online business for moms, click on this link to try out 30-Day Course Moremee.

30-DAY COURSE MOREMEE

If you happen to be a mom seeking an online business opportunity that not only offers convenience but also promises substantial profitability, you're in the right place!

We invite you to explore the 30 Day Course Moremee, a fantastic program that's been tailor-made with moms like you in mind. In today's fast-paced world, juggling the responsibilities of parenthood and career can be quite challenging.

The 30-Day Course Moremee acknowledges the unique needs of mothers and provides a flexible and potentially lucrative online business solution. By simply clicking on this link, you'll embark on a transformative journey that can not only bring financial stability but also allow you to work on your own terms.

The 30 Day Course Moremee is not just another run-of-the-mill online business opportunity. It's a comprehensive program that equips you with the knowledge, tools, and support needed to establish a thriving online venture.

Whether you're a stay-at-home mom or someone with a part-time job, this course can be tailored to fit your schedule and lifestyle. Plus, it's designed to empower you with the skills required to turn your passion or expertise into a profitable online business.

By taking this course, you'll gain access to a wealth of resources, including step-by-step guides, video tutorials, and a supportive community of fellow moms who are on the same journey as you. This sense of belonging can be invaluable as you navigate the world of online entrepreneurship.

So, if you're ready to take the leap into the world of online entrepreneurship, we encourage you to click on this link and explore the 30 Day Course Moremee. It's not just an opportunity; it's a platform designed to empower moms like you to achieve financial independence while balancing the demands of motherhood. Don't miss out on this exciting journey towards a more profitable and flexible future. Your online business success story begins here!

INTRODUCING...

THE 30-DAY
MOREMEE
Blueprint

Everything You Need To Build,
Launch & Sell a 6-Figure Online
Course In Just 30 Days.

Pre Launch SALE

Save 75%

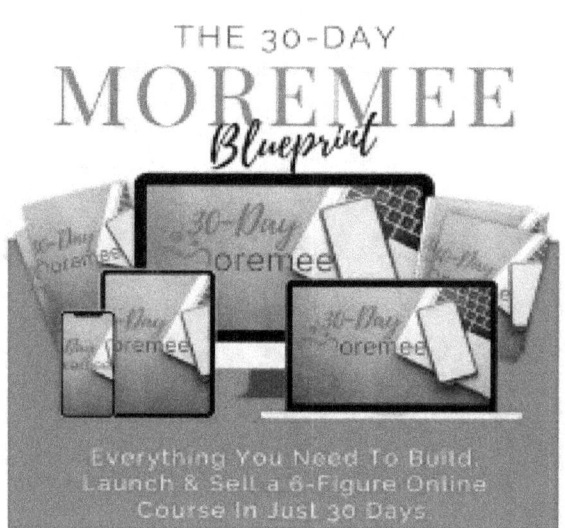

Click on this link to start now